A SECOND PRIMER

OF

CLASSICAL BALLET

(CECCHETTI METHOD)

———

FOR CHILDREN

———

BY

CYRIL W. BEAUMONT

WITH ILLUSTRATIONS

BY

EILEEN MAYO

REVISED AND ENLARGED EDITION

1966

LONDON

C. W. BEAUMONT

75, CHARING CROSS ROAD, W.C.2

PREFACE

Book One of this work is intended to provide a second year's course in classical ballet for a child of average ability taking the customary one class lesson a week.

Book Two provides a succeeding twelve months' training under the same conditions.

Book One and Book Two are also planned to cover respectively all the theoretical knowledge and practical requirements of the Grade II and Grade III syllabi (Revised 1959) of the Classical Ballet Examinations held by the Imperial Society of Teachers of Dancing.

The counts allotted to certain movements are not so much intended as a substitute for music rhythms, as to afford the young student a more definite idea of the desired quality of the particular movement described.

In the naming of *enchaînements* I have purposely introduced into the French technical terminology English words for the number of times a step is to be performed, believing this to be more helpful to young students.

In the preparation of this new edition I desire to record my grateful thanks for the assistance afforded me by Barbara Geoghegan, Carol Hill, and Laura Wilson.

CYRIL W. BEAUMONT

Copyright 1935

Second Impression	.	.	1938
Third Impression	.	.	1943
Fourth Impression	.	.	1945
Fifth Impression	.	.	1947
Sixth Impression	.	.	1950
Seventh Impression	.	.	1953
Eighth Impression	.	.	1954
Ninth Impression	.	.	1956
New and Enlarged Edition	.	.	1960
Eleventh Impression	.	.	1962
Twelfth Impression	.	.	1965
Thirteenth Impression	.	.	1966

Printed in Great Britain by
Cox & Wyman, Ltd., London, Fakenham and Reading

CONTENTS

BOOK ONE—GRADE TWO

THEORY

PRACTICE

EXERCISES AT THE BAR

CENTRE PRACTICE

ADAGE

ALLÉGRO

Contents

BOOK TWO—GRADE THREE

THEORY

PRACTICE

EXERCISES AT THE BAR

CENTRE PRACTICE

Contents

BOOK I: GRADE II

THEORY

I. THE POSITIONS OF THE ARMS

As you know, there are **five** positions of the arms, of which you have already learnt the *first, second,* and *fifth* positions. Now take the *third* and *fourth* positions.

Plate I shows the **third** position of the arms.

The *third* position is formed by one arm being placed as though it formed half the *fifth* position *en bas,* while the other arm is opened slightly to the side. In the drawing the *right* arm is in the *fifth* position and the *left* opened to the side. If the *left* arm is in the *fifth* position and the *right* opened to the side, the arms are also in the *third* position.

The principal faults to guard against in this position are:

Arm in the fifth position.
1. Bringing the hand over the imaginary centre line.
2. Letting the arm hang straight instead of being slightly rounded.
3. Turning the palm to face the audience.
4. Turning the back of the hand to face the audience.

Arm opened to the side.
1. Opening the arm too wide.
2. Not opening the arm sufficiently.
3. Letting the arm hang straight instead of being slightly rounded.
4. Turning the back of the hand to face the audience.
5. Exaggerated turning of the palm of the hand to face the audience.

Plate I shows the **fourth** position of the arms.

There are two *fourth* positions of the arms: one in which one arm is placed in the *second* position, while the other is rounded in front of the body as though it formed half the *fifth* position *en avant*; and one in which one arm is in the *second* position, while the other is rounded above the head as though it formed half the *fifth* position *en haut*. The first of these positions is called the *fourth* position **en avant** (forward), and the second, the *fourth* position **en haut** (above).

In the drawing of the *fourth* position *en avant*, the *right* arm is rounded in front of the body and the *left* arm is in the *second* position. If the *left* arm is rounded in front of the body and the *right* arm is in the *second* position, the arms are also in the *fourth* position *en avant*.

In the drawing of the *fourth* position *en haut*, the *right* arm is raised and the *left* arm is in the *second* position. If the *left* arm is raised and the *right* arm is in the *second* position, the arms are also in the *fourth* position *en haut*.

The principal faults to guard against in the *fourth* position *en avant* are those governing the *second* and *fifth* positions of the arms, for instance:

Arm in the second position.

1.   Dropping the arm below the desired level.
2.   Raising the arm above the desired level.
3.   Dropping the elbow so that the arm becomes V-shaped.
4.   Dropping the wrist.
5.   Turning the hand palm downwards.
6.   Turning the hand palm upwards.
7.   Placing the line of the arm too far forwards.
8.   Placing the line of the arm too far backwards.

Arm in front of the body.

1.   Bringing the hand over the imaginary centre line.
2.   Over-extending the arm so that it is straight, instead of being slightly rounded.
3.   Bringing the hand too close to the body, so that the point of the elbow is visible and the fore-arm almost parallel to the body.
4.   Turning the hand palm upwards.
5.   Turning the hand palm downwards.
6.   Dropping the wrist.

Plate I

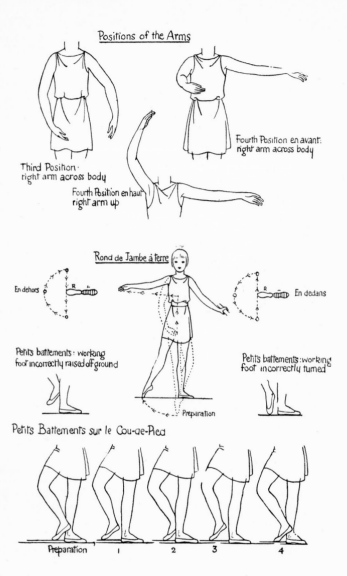

Positions of the Arms

Third Position·
right arm across body

Fourth Position en avant·
right arm across body

Fourth Position en haut·
right arm up

Rond de Jambe à terre

En dehors   R   En dedans

Petits battements: working
foot incorrectly raised off ground

Petits battements: working
foot incorrectly turned

Preparation

Petits Battements sur le Cou-de-Pied

Preparation   1   2   3   4

The principal faults to guard against in the *fourth* position *en haut* are those governing the *second* position and *fifth* position *en haut* of the arms, for instance:

Arm in the second position (see page 10).

Arm above the head.

1.   Over-extending the arm so that it is straight instead of being slightly rounded.

2.   Dropping the arm too far forwards.

3.   Carrying the arm too far backwards.

4.   Turning the palm to face the audience.

5.   Turning the back of the hand to face the audience.

6.   Under-extending the arm so that the point of the elbow is visible.

II. THE FIVE POSITIONS OF THE HEAD

There are **five** principal positions of the head (see Plate VII).

1.   Head **erect**

2.   Head **inclined to one side** (this can be done to either side).

3.   Head **turned to one side** (this can be done to either side).

4.   Head **raised.**

5.   Head **lowered.**

III. THE POSITIONS OF THE BODY

There are **eight** positions of the body, of which you have already learnt three—*à la quatrième devant*, *à la seconde*, and *à la quatrième derrière*. These are comparatively simple because in each of the three positions named, the body faces front, or wall number 5, and in each case the arms are placed in the *second* position, the only difference being in the position of the extended leg.

The remaining five positions are more difficult in that while the body always faces one or other of the two front corners (that is corner No. 1, or corner No. 2), the position of the arms and the extended leg are different, moreover, the head, too, has a special placing.

The names of two of the remaining five positions of the body (see Plate II) are:

4. **croisé devant.**

5. **croisé derrière.**

Croisé devant

Croisé means *crossed*, and *devant*, as you know, means *front*, and so the term *croisé devant* means *crossed front*. The crossing refers to the legs, and, in the position *croisé devant*, it is the leg **nearest the audience** that is pointed *devant*, or extended *sur la pointe tendue*. The feet are in the *fourth* position, *right* foot *front* or *left* foot *front*, as the case may be.

If, therefore, the *right* leg is to be pointed *devant*, the body faces 2, because the foot nearest the audience is the one to be extended. Similarly, if the *left* leg is to be pointed, the body faces 1, because the foot nearest the audience is the one to be extended.

The arms are placed so that one is like half the *fifth* position *en haut* except that it is **opened a little more**, while the other is midway between the *second* position and *first* position, which is called the *demi-seconde* or mid-second position. This position of the arms is called *en attitude*, *right* arm up. The arm that is low or in the *demi-seconde* position is the same as the leg extended. If the *right* leg is pointed, then the *right* arm is in the *demi-seconde* position. The head is slightly inclined towards the arm in the *demi-seconde* position, the eyes looking towards the audience.

In the *demi-seconde* position as used in certain of the eight positions of the body, notice that the PALM of the hand always FACES FRONT. But when the *demi-seconde* position is used in certain steps in *allegro* the palms of the hands are turned INWARDS so that the thumb-nails face the audience (see Plate VI, *glissade devant*).

Examine the drawing of the position *croisé devant* and note that the body faces 2, the head inclines to 1, the *right* leg points to 2, the *left* foot points to 3, the right arm points to 1, and the left arm is to 3.

Plate II

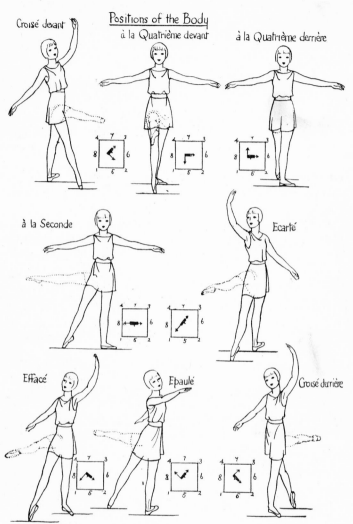

Positions of the Body

Croisé devant

à la Quatrième devant

à la Quatrième derrière

à la Seconde

Ecarté

Effacé

Epaulé

Croisé derrière

The black oblong represents the direction of the body. The short arrow marks the direction of the supporting foot while the long arrow shows the direction of the extended foot.

Croisé derrière

Croisé means crossed, and *derrière*, as you know, means back or behind, so the complete term *croisé derrière* means *crossed behind*. The crossing, as before, refers to the legs, and now it is the leg **furthest away from the audience** that is pointed *derrière*, or extended behind, *sur la pointe tendue*. The feet are in the *fourth* position, *right* foot *back*, or *left* foot *back*, as the case may be.

If the *right* leg is to be pointed *derrière*, the body faces 1, because the leg furthest away from the audience is the one to be extended. If the *left* leg is to be pointed, the body faces 2, because the leg furthest away from the audience is the one to be extended.

The arms are *en attitude*. The arm that is low or in the *demi-seconde* position is the same as the leg extended. If, therefore, the *right* leg is pointed, then the *right* arm is in the *demi-seconde* position. The head is slightly inclined *towards* the arm in the *demi-seconde* position, the eyes looking towards the audience.

Examine the drawing of the position *croisé derrière* and note that the body faces 1, the head inclines to 4, the *right* leg points to 3, the *left* foot points to 2, the *right* arm points to 4, and the *left* arm is to 2.

IV. THE MOVEMENTS IN DANCING

There are **seven** movements in dancing, of which you have learnt three: *plier*, to bend; *sauter*, to jump; and *relever*, to rise. Here are two more:

4. **glisser,** to glide.
5. **tourner,** to turn.

V. THEORY OF THE MOVEMENT OF THE HEAD IN A PIROUETTE

As you proceed with your training you will learn several rules concerning the use of the head, the careful observance of which will do much to help your balance and add grace and charm to your movements and positions.

As a beginning it is a good plan to start to study the use of the head in the *pirouette*. In a *pirouette* the head is the last to leave the audience and the first to return to it.

Stand in the centre of the room and face 5, then, keeping on place and taking small steps on the flat of the feet, turn in four movements to the *right*, keeping your eyes looking as long as possible to 5, then, quickly turn your head to the *right*, so that it again looks to 5, and continue to turn to the *right* for another four movements, which brings you back to your original position. The turn to the right is continuous, without any pause.

See Plate IV for an illustration of the movement of the head.

Practise the same movements turning to the *left*.

PRACTICE

EXERCISES AT THE BAR

In the previous book you learned how to do several exercises at the bar—*pliés, grands battements, battements tendus, battements frappés, relevés* in the 5th position, and *échappés.* Now you will learn some new exercises which are a little more difficult.

GRANDS BATTEMENTS

You have already learned how to do these in four movements. Now perform them quicker, without pausing in the *pointe tendue* position, so that the timing is now "up" on the "&", and close on the count, the rhythm is thus: "& 1", "& 2", "& 3", "& 4". Take particular care always to **slide** the working foot out and in.

BATTEMENTS DÉGAGÉS TO 1st POSITION

Battements dégagés, literally *beatings disengaged,* i.e. *disengaged beatings*

Preparation. Stand erect with the head upright, the *left* hand clasping the *barre,* the *right* arm in the *fifth* position *en bas,* and the feet in the *first* position.

Exercise.

Keep both knees straight and slide the *right* foot to the *second* position, *pointe tendue.* Carry the foot out a little further—keeping the toe pointed well downwards—so that since the body must remain erect, it now rises about four inches off the ground. Lower it to the *second* position, *pointe tendue*, and return it to the *first* position, pressing the heel down well.

Execute several *battements dégagés*, **slowly.**

Remarks.

If we consider the movement as being composed of two measures, the rhythm may be expressed as follows:

Count " & ", as you slide the foot from the *first* position to the *second* position, *pointe tendue*, and release it from the ground.

Count " 1 ", as you lower the foot to the *second* position, and return it to the *first* position.

In Grade III the *battement dégagé* is performed *a tempo*, two *battements dégagés* to the time of one *battement tendu*.

INTRODUCTION TO RONDS DE JAMBE À TERRE

The term *rond de jambe à terre* means *circle of the leg on the ground*. It is an exercise in which one leg is made to describe a series of circular movements on the ground. Such movements are very useful to loosen the hips and turn the leg outwards from the hips, and to help you to keep the front of the toe well back and the heel well forwards. There are two kinds of *ronds de jambe à terre*: those done *en dehors*, or **outwards,** and those done *en dedans*, **or inwards.**

Ronds de Jambe à Terre en Dehors

Preparation. Stand erect with the head upright, the *left* hand clasping the *bar*, the *right* arm in the *fifth* position *en bas*, and the feet in the *first* position.

On preparatory notes of the music:

(a) Raise the *right* arm to the *fifth* position *en avant*.

(b) Open the *right* arm to the *second* position.

Exercise.

1. Slide the *right* foot to the *fourth* position *front, pointe tendue* (Count 1).

2. Sweep the *right* foot outwards along the ground so that it passes to the *second* position, *pointe tendue* (Count 2).

3. Keep the *right* foot, *pointe tendue,* and sweep it outwards along the ground so that it passes to the *fourth* position *back, pointe tendue* (Count 3).

4. Slide the *right* foot forward, gradually lowering the heel, to the *first* position (Count 4).

Repeat the whole exercise.

Ronds de Jambe à Terre en Dedans

Perform the same movement as for **Ronds de jambe à terre en dehors,** but in the reverse manner. The exercise **en dedans** is similarly repeated.

BATTEMENTS FRAPPÉS DOUBLES

Battements frappés doubles, that is to say, *double* striking beatings, are done similarly to ordinary *battements frappés.* The only difference is that the working foot is passed from the *cou-de-pied devant* to the *cou-de-pied derrière,* or from the *cou-de-pied derrière* to the *cou-de-pied devant,* before being extended.

Battements frappés doubles are usually done immediately after a series of *battements frappés,* and, like them, serve to strengthen the instep and toes, and to strengthen and render the muscles elastic.

Preparation. Having done 16[1] *battements frappés* with the *right* foot, you will find that the foot is extended in the *second* position, but with the foot raised slightly off the ground.

[1] This number can be varied in accordance with the pupil's ability.

Exercise. 1. Withdraw the *right* foot *sur le cou-de-pied devant.*

2. Pass the *right* foot *sur le cou-de-pied derrière,* opening from the knee joint. } (Count 1.)

3. Keep the *left* knee straight, and, without moving the *right* thigh and pressing firmly *sur la demi-pointe,* sharply slide the foot out to the *second* position, and then further so that it rises about four inches off the ground. As the foot rises off the ground point the toe well downwards so that the instep is forced outwards (Count 2, 3, 4).

Note. The counts are to show the rhythm of the movement and do not refer to the beats of the music.

Do this exercise 16 times, returning the foot *sur le cou-de-pied devant* and *derrière,* alternately.

Timing. The counts should be spoken crisply.

Remarks. Remember that in *battements frappés doubles,* as in ordinary *battements frappés,* the thigh must be kept steady so that the working leg is pivoted at the knee. Be very careful not to swing or jerk the thigh, to keep the supporting knee straight, and the thigh muscles well drawn up.

The *demi-pointe* of the foot strikes the ground firmly as it rises into the air, and returns *sur le cou-de-pied* without touching the ground. The accent of the movement is when the foot strikes the ground. Take care that this accent is not left out, and that the foot is returned to the correct position *sur le cou-de-pied devant* or *derrière.* The whole movement must be *sharp,* but quite free from any jerkiness.

In ordinary *battements frappés,* one beat, as you know, is counted for withdrawing the foot *sur le cou-de-pied devant* or *derrière* after being extended in the *second* position. In *battements frappés doubles* only one beat is counted, both for withdrawing the foot *sur le cou-de-pied derrière* and passing it *sur le cou-de-pied devant,* or *vice versa,* so that this portion of the movement must now be taken twice as quickly.

Exercise with the Left Foot. Having faced about and changed feet and done the usual 16 *battements frappés* with the left foot, you will find that the foot is extended in the *second* position, but with the foot slightly off the ground. Now do 16 *battements frappés doubles* with the *left* foot.

PETITS BATTEMENTS SUR LE COU-DE-PIED

Petits battements sur le cou-de-pied means *little beatings on the neck of the foot,* and consists in resting one foot *sur le cou-de-pied devant* of the other, and then passing it backwards and forwards from the *cou-de-pied derrière* to the *cou-de-pied devant,* taking the foot out to the side only just enough to pass it behind the supporting leg. As this kind of movement is used in many beating steps this exercise is to prepare you for the execution of *batterie,* which is the French technical term for *beaten steps.*

Preparation. Stand erect with the head upright, the *left* hand clasping the bar, the *right* arm in the *fifth* position, and the feet in the position shown in Plate I. Note that the *right* foot is resting *sur le cou-de-pied devant* of the *left* foot, with the pads of the toes on the ground.

Exercise.
1. Keep the *right* foot relaxed and pass it to the side so that the heel is just a little distance from the back of the supporting ankle.
2. In the same manner pass the *right* foot *sur le cou-de-pied derrière.*
3. Keep the *right* foot relaxed and pass it to the side, so that the heel is just a little distance from the back of the supporting ankle.
4. In the same manner pass the *right* foot *sur le cou-de-pied devant.*

See Plate I for a diagram of the complete movement.

Do this exercise 16 times.

Remarks. For the present it will be sufficient for you to pass the foot slowly backwards and forwards, making each portion of the movement equal. Later on, when you have practised the movement, it will be done with a certain accent.

Remember that the working foot must not be raised off

the ground, and keep the heel well forwards, so that the toe does not turn inwards as it has a tendency to do. The thigh must be kept steady so that the working leg is pivoted at the knee. Take care not to swing or jerk the thigh, to keep the supporting knee straight and the thigh muscles well drawn up.

Lastly, be very careful to keep the supporting knee straight and the thigh muscles well drawn up, and to keep the working foot under control so that the four movements are as regular as clockwork. It is very easy for the working foot to swing out of position and to slip up the supporting leg or below the *cou-de-pied*, and even to swing past the supporting leg, in which case the exercise is useless and a pure waste of time.

Exercise of the Left Foot. Face about and change the feet so that the *left* is resting on the *cou-de-pied* of the *right*, and execute with the *left* foot 16 *petits battements*.

ADAGE AT THE BAR

Preparation. Stand erect with the head upright, the *left* hand clasping the bar, the feet in the *fifth* position. *right* foot *front*, and the *right* arm in the *fifth* position *en bas*.

Exercise.

Développé à la quatrième devant en l'air, with the *right* foot and usual arm movement, rise on to the *left* *demi-pointe* (*relevé*), lower heel again, then bring *right* foot down to the *fourth* position *front*, *pointe tendue*, and back on to the *cou-de-pied devant* with the foot relaxed; lower *right* arm to the *fifth* position *en bas* as you bring the foot *sur le cou-de-pied*.

The whole takes 4 bars of Waltz music.

NOTE. The supporting heel must be lowered before the working leg is lowered to *pointe tendue*.

Repeat the above **à la quatrième derrière en l'air,** then do a **développé à la seconde en l'air,** but omitting the **relevé** ; instead, turn to face the bar, placing both hands upon it, leaving the leg *en arabesque*, and being very careful to keep the hips level and the waist held in.

PORT DE BRAS

As you know there are **eight** exercises on *port de bras*, of which you have already learnt the First and Third exercises. Now take the Second exercise.

NOTE.—The thick upright line means that all the movements beside it are to be done at the same time.

Second Exercise. Stand erect in the centre of the room and face 2, with the head inclined to 3, the feet in the *fifth* position, *right* foot *front*, and the arms in the *fifth* position *en bas*.

Preparation.

(*a*)   Raise the arms to the *fifth* position *en avant* so that they face 2.

(*b*) | Raise the *left* arm upright, slightly curved, and in front of the *left* shoulder so that the elbow faces 2.
Move the *right* arm between the *demi-seconde* position and the *fourth* position *back*, so that it points to 4. The palm of the hand should face downwards.
Bring the head erect and look towards the left hand.

Exercise.

Count

1, 2. | Move the *left* arm downwards and backwards, passing through the *second* position, so that it is extended in the *fourth* position *back*, pointing to 4, the back of the hand to the audience.
Move the *right* arm forwards and upwards, passing through the *second* position, so that it is extended in the *fourth* position *front*, palm of hand turned downwards, pointing to 2.
Incline the head towards 1.
(The arms are in the *second arabesque.*)

NOTE.—When the arms are in the *first* or *second arabesque* the *front* arm is said to be *extended in the fourth position front*, while the rear arm is said to be *extended in the fourth position back*.

3. | Lower the *left* arm to the *first* position, pass it so that it forms one half of the *fifth* position *en bas*, and then raise it so that it forms one half of the *fifth* position *en avant*.
Curve the *right* arm inwards and downwards so that the arms meet in the *fifth* position *en avant*.

4. | Raise the *left* arm upright and in front of the *left* shoulder, so that the elbow faces 2.
Move the *right* arm downwards between the *demi-seconde* position and the *fourth* position *back*, so that it points to 4.
Bring the head erect and look towards the *left* hand.

See Plate III for diagram of the complete movement.

Do this exercise 4 times, without, of course, repeating the preparation.

Timing.   The counts are not to be spoken crisply, but in a singing voice.

Remarks.   In passing the arms from the preparatory position to *en arabesque,* **be very careful to pass through the second position, allowing the palms gradually to face the audience during the change.** As the arms pass from the *second* position to *en arabesque,* gradually turn the palm of the front hand downwards.

In passing the *left* arm from the *first* position to the *fifth* position *en bas,* allow the little finger to brush the skirt in passing. This helps to keep the hand in the correct position.

The arms should be moved in unison and in proportion, so that when one arm has to move further than the other, the arm travelling through the shorter distance should be slightly slowed down in order that the combined movements are completed at the same time. Move the arms from the shoulder and not from the elbow, and avoid any appearance of their being cramped. Again, move them smoothly so that they flow from one position to another.

ADAGE

Adage is a French word derived from the Italian *ad agio,* meaning, *at ease,* or *at leisure.* In dancing, *adage* is the name given to a series of exercises designed to develop grace, sense of line, and balance, particularly when the body is supported on one foot.

Each exercise is divided into a series of complete movements which are numbered according to the order in which they are to be done. A thick upright line means that all the movements beside it are to be done at the same time.

Plate III

Second Port de Bras

Preparation   1   2   3   4

Fourth Port de Bras

Preparation   2   3   4

When you come to do these exercises, you will find that, in passing from one position to another, an arm may have to move through a greater distance than the leg, or the reverse. When this occurs, take care slightly to slow down the arm or leg that moves through a shorter distance, so that the combined movement is completed at the same time.

The most important points to remember in exercises in *adage* are to keep the supporting knee straight and the thigh muscles well drawn up to tighten it; to keep the body lifted off the hips and the stomach muscles drawn in; and so to adjust the hips that, however the working leg moves, they are always level and square to the direction in which you face.

Do not be too anxious to raise your working leg to a full *second* position *en l'air*, or to a full *fourth* position *en l'air*, because the balance and strength to do this must be built up gradually. *It is far more important to maintain a good balance even if the working leg is not fully raised*, because the raising of the working leg to the correct height can be achieved by degrees, whereas a faulty balance will not only spoil all your work, but is extremely difficult to correct.

1st, 2nd, & 3rd ARABESQUES

As you know there are five principal *arabesques*, of which you have learnt the first. Up to the present you have raised the rear leg *pointe tendue*, but, now that you are stronger, it must be raised *en l'air*. We will now take the *first arabesque* in the more difficult position and pass on to the *second* and *third*.

Preparation. Stand erect in the centre of the 100m and face 5, with the head upright, the feet in the *fifth* position, *right* foot *front*, and the arms in the *fifth* position *en bas*.

Exercise.

1. *Développé à la seconde en l'air* with the *right* foot.
As the *right* toe rises to the side of the left knee—
Raise the arms to the *fifth* position *en avant* (Count 1).
As the *right* foot is extended to the *second* position *en l'air*—
Open the arms to the *second* position (Count 2, 3, 4).

2. | Turn the body sideways to face 6, leaving the *right* leg pointing to 8.

Turn both hands palms downwards and extend the fingers, then slightly raise the *left* hand so that the finger-tips are in a line with the centre of the space between the eyes. The *right* arm should be slightly lowered so that the arms are in one straight line.

Bring the *left* heel slightly forwards (Count 5—8).

3. | Move the *left* arm downwards and backwards, passing through the *second* position, so that the arms are in one straight line.

Move the *right* arm forwards and upwards, passing through the *second* position, so that the extremity of the **right** hand is now in a line with the centre of the space between the eyes.

Slightly incline and turn the head to the *right*. (Count 9—12.)

This is the **second** *arabesque*.

4. | Slightly lower the *right* arm to the *fifth* position *en avant*.

Move the *left* arm forwards and upwards, passing through the *first* position, and round it to the *fifth* position *en avant*.

Then raise and extend both arms *en arabesque* so that the finger-tips of the *left* arm are in a line with the centre of the space between the eyes, while the *right* arm is in a line with the shoulder.

Turn the head to face 6 (Count 13—15).

This is the **third** *arabesque*.

5. | Close the *right* foot to the *fifth* position *back*, and turn the body to face 5.

Lower the arms to the *fifth* position *en bas* (Count 16).

NOTE.—The counts are in bars, the whole exercise taking 16 bars of Waltz time.

See Plate IV for diagram of the complete exercise.

Repeat the exercise to the opposite side, extending the *left* foot.

Remarks. The raised hand in an *arabesque* should be turned slightly outwards. Be careful that the hand is held

Plate IV

First Arabesque

Second Arabesque

Third Arabesque

Conclusion

Fourth Arabesque

Fifth Arabesque

Positions of Head

Corresponding positions of Feet

Demonstration of Movement of Head in a Pirouette, turning sur Place in eight steps

palm downwards and not with the palm upright in the manner of a policeman stopping traffic. In the second, third, and fourth movements, when the body is turned sideways, be sure to hold the hips and shoulders square to the line of direction, keeping the chest raised and broadened, the knees straight, and the thigh muscles well drawn up.

GRAND PLIÉ IN FIFTH POSITION

Preparation. Stand erect in the centre of the room and face 2, with the head inclined to the *left*, the feet in the *fifth* position, *right* foot *front*, and the arms in the *fifth* position *en bas*.

1. Do a full *plié* taking two counts down, opening arms to the *demi-seconde* position, and two counts up, closing the arms in the *fifth* position *en bas*.

2. Open the *left* foot to the *second* position, *pointe tendue*, and close in the *fifth* position *front*, turning to face 1, with the head inclined to the *right*.

Repeat the whole facing 1.

The exercise takes 4 bars of *Cinq Relevés* music.

PREPARATION FOR RELEVÉS IN ADAGE

Preparation. Stand erect in the centre of the room and face 5, with the feet in the *fifth* position, *right* foot *front*, and the arms in the *fifth* position *en bas*.

Using the *right* leg, **développé** and **relevé** as described in the work at the *barre*, **à la quatrième devant, à la seconde, à la quatrième derrière,** and again **à la seconde,** closing the *right* foot behind in the *fifth* position, ready to repeat the whole exercise with the *left* leg.

The *développé* with *relevé* is counted as follows:

On "1" the foot comes to the *cou-de-pied*.
On "2" the foot comes to the side of the knee.
On "3" the leg is extended.
On "&" there is a slight *relevé*.
On "4" the heel is again lowered.
On "&" the foot is lowered to the ground, *pointe tendue*, ready to be withdrawn *sur le cou-de-pied*, etc.

The *développés* should be **as full and as smooth as possible.**

c

ALLÉGRO

In the previous book you learned how to do ten steps—
*posé en avant, temps levé, changement, coupé dessous, coupé
dessus, jeté devant, jeté derrière, grand pas de chat, échappé
sauté à la seconde*, and *échappé sur les demi-pointes*. Here are
some new steps which you will find a little more difficult.

All the movements described have been arranged to
begin with the *right* foot. But, as soon as you have learned
to do them, so you should practise them with the *left* foot,
merely reversing the descriptions, that is to say, reading
left for *right*, or *right* for *left*, as the case may be.

Do not forget that the most important qualities to aim at
in *allégro* are lightness, smoothness, and *ballon*, which, you
will remember, means bounciness, that easy rising and
falling which you notice in a bouncing, india-rubber ball.

In coming to the ground after a spring or a leap, always
allow the knees to bend. Remember that the tips of your
toes should be the first to reach the ground, then the sole,
and lastly the heel. In rising from the ground the foot
moves in the reverse order. That is to say, the heel is the
first to leave the ground, then the sole, and lastly the tips of
the toes.

ASSEMBLÉ SOUTENU DESSUS

Assemblé is short for *pas assemblé*, meaning *assembling* or
bringing-together step. *Soutenu* means sustained. Thus the
whole sentence means *sustained assembling-step—over*.

Preparation. Stand erect in the centre of the room and
face 5, with the head upright, the feet in the *fifth* position,
left foot *front*, and the arms in the *fifth* position *en bas*.

Execution.

1. (a) *Demi-pliez* on both feet and slide the *right* foot
to the *second* position, *en l'air*.
Open the arms to the *demi-seconde* position.

Exactly as the *right* foot rises to the *second* position,
en l'air—
Leap upwards into the air off the *left* foot.
Incline the head to 8.
While the body is in the air—

(*b*) Bend both knees slightly and bring together the flat of the toes of both feet.

(*c*) Come to the ground—allowing the knees to bend with the feet in the *fifth* position, *right* foot *front*, and lower the heels to the ground, then—
Lower the arms to the *fifth* position *en bas*.
Straighten the knees.
Do this step 4 times.

NOTE.—In the execution of a series of this step, the knees must be straightened each time before recommencing the step.

This step travels **forwards**; but it can also be done travelling **backwards,** when it is called *assemblé soutenu dessous*, because the foot that is in front passes *dessous* or *under* the other foot. The *assemblé soutenu dessous* differs then only from the step described in that the leg opened to the *second* position *en l'air* starts from the **front** and is **closed behind,** while the head is inclined **away** from the working foot.

PAS DE BOURRÉE DEVANT

Pas de bourrée means *bourrée step*, Bourrée being the name of an old dance.

Preparation. Stand erect in the centre of the room and face 5, with the head upright, the feet in the *fifth* position, *left* foot *front*, and the arms in the *fifth* position *en bas*.

Execution.

1. *Demi-pliez* on both feet and slide the *right* foot—straightening the knee—to the *second* position, *pointe tendue*; then open the leg a little further so that the *pointe* is about three inches off the ground.
Open the arms to the *second* position.

2 (*a*) Bring the *right* foot to the *fifth* position *front*, both feet *sur les demi-pointes*.

(*b*) Immediately the *right* foot meets the *left* foot, open the latter to the *second* position, *sur la demi-pointe*.

C*

3. | Carry the *right* foot in front of the *left*, so that the *pointe* is just off the ground and immediately— Lower both heels to the ground and *demi-pliez* on both feet.

Arms.

On the *dégagé* the arms open to the *second* position as stated.

On the next three movements the *right* arm is gradually brought across the body as shown in Plate V. Notice that the right palm gradually turns face downwards.

The head is inclined to the *right*.

See Plate V for diagram of the complete movement.

Do this step 4 times, commencing with alternate feet.

NOTE.—This step can also be started with the *right* foot in *front*, sliding it to the *second* position and closing it in *front* of the left, as when beginning with the *left* foot *front*. That is, the *battement dégagé*, as this sliding-out movement is termed, can be started from the *fifth* position *front* or the *fifth* position *back*. *Battement dégagé* means *disengaging beating*. *Dégagé* is short for *battement dégagé*.

PAS DE BOURRÉE DERRIÈRE

Preparation. Stand erect in the centre of the room and face 5, with the head upright, the feet in the *fifth* position, *right* foot *front*, and the arms in the *fifth* position *en bas*.

Execution.

1. | *Demi-pliez* on both feet and slide the *right* foot— straightening the knee—to the *second* position, *pointe tendue*; then open the leg a little further so that the *pointe* is about three inches from the ground. Open the arms to the *second* position.

2. (a) Bring the *right* foot to the *fifth* position *back*, both feet *sur les demi-pointes*.

(b) Immediately the *right* foot meets the *left* foot, open the latter to the *second* position, *sur la demi-pointe*.

Plate V

Pas de Bourrée devant

Audience   Audience

Pas de Bourrée devant

- Right foot
- Left
- Right foot sur la demi pointe
- Left
- foot off ground
- track of right foot
- left

Pas de Bourrée derrière

Pas de Bourrée dessus

Pas de Bourrée dessous

3. | Carry the *right* foot behind the *left*, so that the *pointe* is just off the ground.
Incline the head away from the *right* foot as it closes behind. and immediately—
Lower both heels to the ground and *demi-pliez* on both feet.

Arms.

The arms remain in the *second* position throughout.
See Plate V for diagram of the complete movement.
Do this step 4 times, commencing with alternate feet.

NOTE.—This step can also be started with the *right* foot *back*, using it for the *dégagé*.

CHASSÉ

Chassé is short for *pas chassé*, that is *chasing step*.

Preparation. Stand erect in the centre of the room and face 5, with the head upright, the feet in the *fifth* position, *right* foot *front*, and the arms in the *fifth* position *en bas*.

Execution.

1. | *Demi-pliez* on both feet and, keeping the weight equally distributed, slide the *right* foot—keeping the knee bent—to the *second* position.
Open the arms to the *demi-seconde* position.
Incline the head to 8.

Do this step also to the *fourth* position *front*, and *fourth* position *back*.

See Plate VI for a diagram of the movement.

NOTE.—This movement can also be executed in all the positions of the body.

ECHAPPÉ SUR LES DEMI-POINTES

Echappé is short for *temps echappé*, meaning *escaping movement*.

Preparation. Stand erect in the centre of the room and face 5, with the feet in the *fifth* position, *right* foot *front*, and the arms in the *fifth* position *en bas*.

Execution.

1. *Demi-pliez* on both feet and, with a slight spring, instantaneously—

   > Open the feet *sur les demi-pointes* in the second position. Open the arms to the *demi-seconde* position.

2. With a slight spring, return to the *fifth* position, without changing the feet.
   Lower the arms to the *fifth* position *en bas*.

Do this exercise 8 times, keeping the feet in the same position as at the beginning, or changing them so that first the *right* foot is *front*, then the *left*, and so alternately.

Remarks.   Remember that the term *sur les demi-pointes* here means three-quarter points, so that the insteps should be forced well outwards and the heels raised as high as possible, bending the toes.

SOUSSUS

Soussus means *under-over*. You will notice that it is exactly the same as a *relevé* in the *fifth* position—but *travelled forwards*.

Preparation.   Stand erect in the centre of the room and face 2, with the head inclined to 3, the feet in the *fifth* position, *right* foot *front*, and the arms in the *fifth* position *en bas*.

Execution.

1. *Demi-pliez* on both feet and with a slight spring forwards—

   > (*a*) Rise on the three-quarter points, drawing the toes closely together and forcing the heels well forwards.
   > Raise the arms a little below the *fifth* position *en avant*, with the palms half turned upwards, using the wrists only.

   > (*b*) With a slight spring, lower the heels in the *fifth* position.
   > Lower the arms to the *fifth* position *en bas*.

Plate VI

Developpés

Pas de Bourrée dessous
Ending

Chasse using right foot

a

b

a

b

Glissade devant

Audience   &   Audience

Plan of Glissade devant

○ · Right foot
○ · Left
· Foot off ground
→→· Track of right foot
→→→ · left ·

Plan of Glissade derrière

Audience

Plan of Glissade dessous

Audience

Plan of Glissade dessus

GLISSADE DEVANT

Glissade, derived from the verb *glisser, to glide,* means *gliding step.*

Preparation. Stand erect in the centre of the room and face 5, with the head upright, the feet in the *fifth* position, *right* foot *front,* and the arms in the *fifth* position *en bas.*

Execution.

1. *Demi-pliez* on both feet and slide the *right* foot, pressing it strongly against the ground, to the *second* position and then a little *further* until the *pointe* is raised three inches from the ground.
   Open the arms to the *demi-seconde* position.
   Incline the head to the *right.*

2. Spring slightly on the *right* foot, raising the *left* foot three inches from the ground, pointing the toe well downwards, and carry it in behind the right heel, at the same time bending the *right* knee, and *immediately* lower the *left* heel to the ground, allowing the knee to bend.
   Lower the arms to the *fifth* position *en bas.*

See Plate VI for diagram of the complete movement.

Do this step 4 or 8 times.

NOTE.—In a *glissade* it is the first foot that slides, while the second is just lifted and closed in place. This step should be done very smoothly to avoid any jerkiness when transferring the weight from the left foot to the right.

GLISSADE DERRIÈRE

Preparation. Stand erect in the centre of the room and face 5, with the head upright, the feet in the *fifth* position, *left* foot *front,* and the arms in the *fifth* position *en bas.*

Execution.

1. *Demi-pliez* on both feet and slide the *right* foot, pressing it strongly against the ground, to the *second* position and then a little further until the *pointe* is raised three inches from the ground.
   Open the arms to the *demi-seconde* position.
   Incline the head to the *left.*

2. | Spring slightly on the *right* foot, raising the *left* foot three inches from the ground, pointing the toe well downwards, and carry it in front of the *right* heel, at the same time bending the *right* knee, and *immediately*—
Lower the *left* heel to the ground, allowing the knee to bend.
Lower the arms to the *fifth* position *en bas.*

Do this step 4 or 8 times.

See Plate VI for a diagram of the movement.

JETÉ DEVANT

Jeté is short for *pas jeté*, meaning *step thrown*, that is, *throwing step*. The adverb *devant* (front) implies that the **working** foot is closed in *front*.

Preparation.   Stand erect in the centre of the room, and face 5, with the feet in the *fifth* position, *left* foot *front*, and the arms in the *fifth* position *en bas.*

Execution.

1. | *Demi-pliez* on both feet.
Execute a small *battement frappé* with the *right* foot.

2. Spring off the *left* foot and come to the ground on the *right* foot, allowing the knee to bend, in front of the position vacated by the *left* foot.
As the *right* foot comes to the ground—
Raise the *left* foot *sur le cou-de-pied derrière.*
Incline the head to the *right*.

NOTE.—The arms remain in the same position throughout.

Do this step 8 times. To recommence, repeat, using the *left* foot, then follow with the right foot, and so on alternately. There should be *no break* between the *jetés*. In the execution of a series of this step, the *demi-plié* on the supporting leg will be omitted after the first *jeté*, since this leg will be bent already.

JETÉ DERRIÈRE

The addition of *derrière* (*behind*) implies that the **working** foot is closed at the *back*.

Preparation. Stand erect in the centre of the room and face 5, with the feet in the *fifth* position, *left* foot *front*, and the arms in the *fifth* position *en bas*.

Execution.

1. *Demi-pliéz* on both feet.
   Execute a small *battement frappé* with the *left* foot.

2. Spring off the *right* foot and come to the ground on the *left* foot, allowing the knee to bend, at the back of the position vacated by the *right* foot.
   As the *left* foot comes to the ground—
   Raise the *right* foot *sur le cou-de-pied devant*.

NOTE.—The arms remain in the same position throughout.

Do this step 8 times. To recommence, repeat with the *right* foot, then follow with the *left* foot, and so on alternately. There should be no break between the *jetés*. In the execution of a series of this step, the *demi-plié* on the supporting leg will be omitted after the first *jeté*, since this leg will be bent already.

ENCHAÎNEMENTS

Enchaînement means *enchainment* or *linking*, and is a linking together or combination of two or more steps. In a way it is not unlike joining several words together to form a sentence.

Here, then, are four *enchaînements* or sentences in dancing:

Three Echappés (sans changer)—soussus. The whole executed *croisé*.

This *enchaînement* is always done on an imaginary line connecting the two opposite corners of the room, that is to say:

1. On the line 4—2, travelling to 2.
2. On the line 3—1, travelling to 1.

Preparation.   Stand erect in the centre of the room and face 2, with the head upright, the feet in the *fifth* position, *right* foot *front*, and the arms in the *fifth* position *en bas.*

Execution.

Do three *échappés sur les demi-pointes*, closing each time to the *fifth* position, *right* foot *front*, and each time opening the arms to *demi-seconde* position and closing them in the *fifth* position *en bas.*

Without stopping, do one *soussus*, remembering to raise the arms to the *fifth* position *en avant* and close them in the *fifth* position *en bas.*

The head is inclined to the back foot throughout and raised a little for the *soussus.*

The term *sans changer* means *without changing* and implies that the feet are to be kept in the same relative position as at the beginning of the step; so, if the feet are in the *fifth* position, *right* foot *front*, the *right* foot closes *front* each time.

Chassé, coupé, chassé, temps levé en troisième arabesque.

Preparation.   Stand erect near 7 and face 5, with the head upright, the feet in the *fifth* position, *right* foot *front*, and the arms in the *fifth* position *en bas.*

Execution.

Do a *chassé* with the *right* foot to the *fourth* position *front*; *coupé dessous* with the *left* foot; repeat *chassé* with the *right* foot, raising the arms to the *fifth* position *en avant*; *temps léve* on the *right* foot in *arabesque*, extending arms *en troisième arabesque*, *right* arm up, head inclined to *right.*

This *enchaînement* is done on an imaginary line 3—1 travelling to 1.

Repeat the whole on the *left* foot, on the line 4—2, travelling to 2.

Three glissades (sans changer) and one changement

Preparation.   Stand erect near 8 and face 5, with the head upright, the feet in the *fifth* position, *right* foot *front* and the arms in the *fifth* position *en bas.*

Execution.

Do three *glissades derrière* with the *left* foot, opening the arms to the *demi-seconde* position on each *glissade* (head inclined to *right*), and travelling towards 6, followed by one *changement*, head inclined to *left*.

Repeat the whole with the *right* foot, travelling towards 8.

This exercise can also be done with three *glissades devant* in place of three *glissades derrière*.

Turns in fifth position en diagonale.

Preparation. Stand erect near 3 and facing 2, with the head turned to 1, the feet in the *fourth* position, *right* foot *pointe tendue*, and the arms in *fourth* position *en avant*, *right* arm *front*.

Execution.

1. *Demi-rond de jambe à terre en dehors* with the *right* foot, allowing the *left* knee to bend.
   Open the *right* arm to the *second* position.

2. Spring on to the *right* foot, allowing the knee to bend. Extend the *left* foot to the *second* position, with the foot just off the ground, turning to the *right*, stil looking towards 1.

3. Close the *left* foot to the *fifth* position *front*, with a *relevé sur les demi-pointes*, turning to the *right*, at the same time changing the position of the feet, bringing the arms to between the *fifth* position *en bas* and the *fifth* position *en avant*, the head sharply brought round to face 1.

4. Drop in the *fifth* position, *right* foot *front*, allowing the knees to bend, facing 2.
   This turn should be done in a series, repeating the preparation each time.

BOOK TWO: GRADE III

THEORY

I. THE POSITIONS OF THE BODY

You have already learnt five of the eight positions of the body. The remaining three (see Plate II) are:

6. **effacé,**
7. **épaulé.**
8. **écarté.**

Effacé

Effacé means *shaded*, and in this position the feet are not crossed. It is as though you stood facing 5, with the feet in the *fourth* position, *right* foot *front* or *left* foot *front* as the case may be, and then shaded the body by turning in the same position to face the corner nearest the extended leg. In the drawing the *right* leg is extended and so the body is turned to face 1.

The arms are placed *en attitude, left* arm up. The arm that is low, or in the *demi-seconde* position, is the same as the leg extended. If, therefore, the *right* leg is pointed *front*, the *right* arm is in the *demi-seconde* position. The head is inclined *away* from the arm in the *demi-seconde* position.

Examine the drawing of the position *effacé* and note that the body faces 1, the head inclines to 2, the right leg points to 1, the left foot points to 2, the right arm points to 4, and the left arm to 2.

Épaulé

Épaulé means *shouldered,* and this position is like an *arabesque,* actually the **second** *arabesque,* with the body facing one or other of the two front corners. The feet are in the *fourth* position, *right* foot *back* or *left* foot *back,* as the case may be.

If the *right* leg is pointed *en arabesque,* the body faces 2 for it is the leg nearest the audience that is extended. If the *left* leg is pointed back, the body faces 1.

The arms are in the second *arabesque,* that is, if the *right* leg is pointed back, the *right* arm is extended to the front and the *left* arm extended to the back. The head is **inclined and slightly turned** to the same side as the extended leg.

Examine the drawing of the position *épaulé* and note that the body faces 2, the head inclines to 1, the *right* leg points to 4, the *left* foot points to 3, the *right* arm points to 2, and the *left* arm to 4.

Écarté

Écarté means *separated,* and in this position the arms and legs are extended in the same line, on the diagonal 1—3, if the body faces 2, or on the diagonal 2—4, if the body faces 1. Here the feet are in the *second* position. If the *right* leg is extended to 1, the *left* foot is pointed to 3.

The arms are placed *en attitude.* The arm that is low or in the *demi-seconde* position is the one **opposite to the extended leg,** and forms the only exception to the rule, when the arms are so placed. The head is turned to face the same corner as that to which the leg is extended.

Examine the drawing of the position *écarté* and note that the body faces 2, the head turns to face 1, the *right* leg points to 1, the *left* points to 3, the *left* arm points to 3, and the *right* arm to 1.

Some Aids to Learning the Eight Positions of the Body

When you have carefully examined the drawings of the eight positions and compared them with the foregoing descriptions, try and make each position in turn. A good plan is to stand on the left foot and use the right as the working leg. Then move the right leg, just as though you were marking all the points of a compass, through the following positions and in the order given:

1. *croisé devant*, pointing to Corner No. 2.
2. *à la quatrième devant*, pointing to Wall No. 5.
3. *écarté*, pointing to Corner No. 1.
4. *effacé*, pointing to Corner No. 1.
5. *à la seconde*, pointing to Wall No. 8.
6. *épaulé*, pointing to Corner No. 4.
7. *à la quatrième derrière*, pointing to Wall No. 7.
8. *croisé derrière*, pointing to Corner No. 3.

Practise these several times. Do not at first pay too great attention to all the details of the arm positions; extend the arms from the shoulders and try to get the correct line of the arms. For instance, in *croisé devant* the arms will be as in the *second* position, but with the *left* arm tilted upwards and the *right* correspondingly down. In *à la quatrième devant* the arms will be level. In *écarté* the *right* arm will be tilted upwards and the *left* arm correspondingly down. When you feel confident regarding the position of both arms and legs, then let the raised arm be rounded correctly. Last of all, add the correct placing of the head in accordance with each position.

The following notes will help you to remember the principal differences between the five difficult positions of the body:

Wall and corner numbers.

1. All face corner 1 or corner 2.

Legs.

1. *Croisé devant* and *effacé* have the feet in the **fourth** position, **extended leg front.**
2. *Croisé derrière* and *épaulé* have the feet in the **fourth** position, **extended leg back.**
3. In *écarté* the **extended leg** is in the **second** position.
4. In *croisé devant*, and *épaulé*, the **extended leg** is that **nearest the audience.**
5. In *croisé derrière* and *effacé* the **extended leg** is that **furthest away from the audience.**

NOTE.—All the positions can be taken with the body supported on the *right* leg and the *left* extended. For the present it will be sufficient for you to place the extended leg *sur la pointe tendue.* Later on, however, as your strength develops, you will be able to do these positions with the extended leg raised to the level of the hip.

II. THE MOVEMENTS IN DANCING

There are **seven** movements in dancing, of which you have learnt five. Here are the remaining two:

6. **élancer,** to dart.

7. **étendre,** to stretch.

Should you discover any difficulty in remembering all the seven movements, you will find it helpful to commit to memory the word **pergset,** which is formed from the first letter of each of the seven French words: **p**lier, to bend; **é**tendre, to stretch; **r**elever, to rise; **g**lisser, to glide; **s**auter, to jump; **é**lancer, to dart; **t**ourner, to turn.

PRACTICE
EXERCISES AT THE BAR

BATTEMENTS DÉGAGÉS

You have learned to do these slowly, now perform them *à tempo,* that is, two to the time of one *battement tendu.*

RONDS DE JAMBE À TERRE
Ronds de Jambe à Terre en Dehors

Preparation. Stand erect with the head upright, the *left* hand clasping the bar, the *right* arm in the *fifth* position, and the feet in the *fifth* position, *right* foot *front.*

1. *Demi-pliez* on both feet, keeping the heels firmly on the ground, and slide the *right* foot to the *fourth* position *front, pointe tendue.* Raise the *right* arm as if it formed half of the *fifth* position *en avant.* Notice that the *right* knee gradually straightens, but keep the *left* knee bent (Count 1.)

NOTE.—The *fourth* position in *ronds de jambe à terre* will be a little difficult for you at first, since it differs from the customary *fourth* position, which, as you know, is like the feet in the *third* position, but separated by the space of one foot. The *fourth* position here is with the feet in the *first* position but separated by the space of a foot, forwards or backwards, according as the foot is in the *fourth* position *front* or the *fourth* position *back*. This *fourth* position is known as an **open** *fourth* position.

> 2. | Sweep the *right* foot outwards along the ground so that it passes to the *second* position, *pointe tendue*. Gradually straighten the *left* knee. Gradually open the *right* arm to the *second* position (Count 2).

NOTE.—Be careful to open the right arm gradually so that it follows the direction of the moving foot.

> 3. Keep the foot *pointe tendue*, and sweep it outwards along the ground so that it passes to the *fourth* position *back*, *pointe tendue* (Count &).

Exercise.

Slide the *right* foot forwards, gradually lowering the heel, to the *first* position, then, gradually raising the heel, slide the foot to the *fourth* position *front*, *pointe tendue*, and sweep it outwards and inwards along the ground so that it passes to the *second* position, *pointe tendue*, and then to the *fourth* position *back*, *pointe tendue* (Count 1 as the foot passes through the *first* position).

The complete half-moon traced by the outward sweep of the foot, commencing from the *first* position, to *fourth* position *front*, *pointe tendue*, to *second* position, *pointe tendue*, to *fourth* position *back*, *pointe tendue*, to *first* position, is termed a *rond de jambe à terre en dehors*. The strong accent occurs as the foot passes through the **first** position.

See Plate I for a diagram of the complete movement.

Do this exercise 8 times. At the conclusion do not end in the *first* position, but open the foot to the *fourth* position, *front*, *pointe tendue*.

Ronds de Jambe à Terre en Dedans

Describe the same movement as for *ronds de jambe à terre en dehors*, but in the reverse manner. That is, withdraw the *right* foot, gradually lowering the heel, to the *first* position, then gradually raising the heel, slide the foot to the *fourth* position *back, pointe tendue*, and sweep it inwards along the ground so that it passes to the *second* position, *pointe tendue*, then to the *fourth* position *front, pointe tendue* (Count 1 as the foot passes through the *first* position.)

The complete half-moon traced by the inward sweep of the foot, as it passes from the *first* position to *fourth* position *back, pointe tendue*, to *second* position, *pointe tendue*, to *fourth* position *front, pointe tendue*, to *first* position, is termed *rond de jambe à terre en dedans*.

See Plate I for a diagram of the complete movement.

Do this exercise 8 times.

On count 8 (the 8th *rond de jambe à terre en dedans* made by the *right* foot) close the *right* foot in the *fifth* position *front*, then—

1. *Demi-pliez* on both feet, keeping the heels firmly on the ground, and slide the *right* foot—straightening the knee—to the *fourth* position *front, pointe tendue*. Raise the *right* arm to form one half of the *fifth* position *en avant* (Count &).

   NOTE.   The *left* knee remains bent.

2. *Grand rond de jambe à terre en dehors*[1] with the *right* foot. That is—

   Move the *right* foot from the *fourth* position *front, pointe tendue*, to the *fourth* position back, *pointe tendue*, passing through the *second* position, *pointe tendue*.

   As the *right* foot passes from the *fourth* position *front, pointe tendue*, to the *second* position, *pointe tendue*—

   Open the *right* arm to the *second* position (Count 1).

   As the *right* foot passes from the *second* position, *pointe tendue*, to the *fourth* position *back, pointe tendue*—Incline the head to the *left*.

[1] *Grand rond de jambe à terre en dedans* is done by moving the foot in the opposite direction.

D

3. *Grand rond de jambe à terre en dedans* with the *right* foot.

As the right foot passes from the *second* position, *pointe tendue*, to the *fourth* position *front*, *pointe tendue*—

Incline the head to the *right*.

4. Close the *right* foot to *fifth* position *front* (Count 3.)
Bring the *right* arm to one half of the *fifth* position *en bas*.
Bring the head erect.

5. *Relevé sur les demi-pointes* (Count &, 1).

6. (*a*) Turn on the balls of the feet towards the bar until the body faces in the opposite direction.
Clasp the bar with the *right* hand.
Raise the *left* arm to form one half of the *fifth* position *en avant* (Count 2).
(*b*) Open the *left* arm to the *second* position.
Turn and incline the head to the *left* (Count 3).

Timing.　The counts are not to be spoken crisply, but in a singing voice.

Remarks.　In the execution of *ronds de jambe à terre*, keep both knees straight, draw up the thigh muscles and force the heel of the working foot well forwards. Take great care that the toe of the working foot does not rise off the ground, and that it does not pass beyond the *fourth* position *front* or the *fourth* position *back*. Also be careful that the half-moon described by the working foot is uniform, and not the front half larger than the rear half, or the reverse.

Exercise of the Left Foot.　Lower the feet in the *fifth* position and repeat the whole exercise with the *left* foot.

PETITS BATTEMENTS SUR LE COU-DE-PIED

You have learned to do *petits battements* in four slow equal movements. Now you must practise to do them quicker, but with a slight **accent** on the **front,** that is, as the foot passes *sur le cou-de-pied devant*. The working foot must not be moved more than is sufficient to pass the heel behind.

Preparation.　Stand erect with the head upright, the *left* hand clasping the bar, the *right* arm in the *fifth* position, and the feet in the position shown in Plate I. Note that the *right* foot is resting *sur le cou-de-pied devant* of the *left* foot. with the pads of the toes on the ground.

Do 16 *petits battements* in the manner described above, finishing with the foot *sur le cou de-pied derrière*.

ADAGE AT THE BAR

Preparation. Stand erect with the head upright, the *left* hand clasping the bar, the feet in the *fifth* position, *right* foot *front*, and the *right* arm in the *fifth* position *en bas*.

Exercise.

1. **Développé à la quatrième devant en l'air,** with the *right* foot.
   Raise the *right* arm to the *fifth* position *en avant*.

2. **Grand rond de jambe en dehors** with the *right* foot.
   Open the *right* arm to the *second* position.

3. Bring the *right* toe to the side of the *left* knee.
   Lower the *right* arm to the *fifth* position *en bas*.

4. **Développé à la seconde en l'air** with the *right* foot.
   Open the *right* arm to the *second* position, passing through the *fifth* position *en avant*.

5. Turn to the *left* and face bar, placing both hands upon it, and leaving *right* leg *en arabesque*.

6. Bring *right* leg *en attitude*.

7. *Relevé* on the *left* foot.

   The whole takes 16 bars of Waltz tempo.

CENTRE PRACTICE

Centre practice is the name given to a group of exercises similar to those performed at the bar, but carried out in the centre of the room, so that you are deprived of the assistance of the bar. The purpose of these exercises is to help you to acquire uprightness and balance. For the present it will be sufficient for you to practise *grands battements* and *battements tendu*.

Do not forget the rules governing exercises in *adage* and so remember to keep the supporting knee straight and the thigh muscles well drawn up to tighten it; to keep the body lifted off the hips and the stomach muscles drawn in; and to keep the hips level and square to the direction in which you face.

PORT DE BRAS

As you know there are eight exercises on *port de bras*, of which you have already learnt the first, second and third; now take the fourth exercise.

Fourth Exercise. Stand erect in the centre of the room and face 2, with the head inclined to 3, the feet in the *fifth* position, *right* foot *front*, and the arms in the *fifth* position *en bas*.

Preparation.

(*a*) Raise the arms to the *fifth* position *en avant*, then—
(*b*) Raise the *right* arm to form one half of the *fifth* position *en haut*, but a little more open and so that the elbow faces 1.
       Move the *left* arm to the *demi-seconde* position so that it points to 3. (The palm of the hand faces *front*.)

Exercise.

Count

1, 2. Raise the *left* arm to form one half of the *fifth* position *en haut*, but a little more open, and so that the elbow faces 3.
       Move the *right* arm to the *demi-seconde* position so that it points to 1.
       Incline the head to 1

NOTE.—If this movement is done and timed correctly there is a *definite moment* when the arms, in passing to their respective places, form the **second** position.

3. Bring the arms to the *fifth* position *en bas*.

NOTE.—The arms must move at the same time and arrive at the correct position together.

4. | Incline the head to 3.
Raise the arms as at the beginning of the exercise, so that the *right* arm forms one half of the *fifth* position *en haut* with the elbow facing 1, while the *left* arm is in the *demi-seconde* position, pointing to 3.

See Plate III for diagram of the complete movement.

Do this exercise 4 times, without, of course, repeating the preparation.

Timing. The counts are not to be spoken crisply, but in a singing voice. Face 1 with the head inclined to 2, the feet in the *fifth* position, *left* foot *front*, and the arms in the *fifth* position *en bas*, and repeat the Second and Fourth Exercises in Port de Bras, reading *right* for *left* and *vice versa*, while the wall numbers stated above will correspond to those directly opposite.

GRANDS BATTEMENTS

Preparation. Stand erect in the centre of the room and face 5, with the head erect, the feet in the *fifth* position, *right* foot *front*, and the arms in the *fifth* position *en bas*.

Exercise. Raise the arms to the *fifth* position *en avant* and open them to the *second* position, then execute with the *right* foot—

1. Four *grands battements à la quatrième devant en l'air*.

2. Four *grands battements à la seconde*, closing in the *fifth* position *front* and *fifth* position *back*, alternately.

3. Four *grands battements à la quatrième derrière en l'air*.

Exercise with the Left Foot. Keep the last position and repeat the whole exercise with the *left* foot.

BATTEMENTS TENDUS

Preparation. Stand erect in the centre of the room and face 5, with the head erect, the feet in the *fifth* position, *right* foot *front*, and the arms in the *fifth* position *en bas*. Open the *right* foot to the *second* position, *pointe tendue*.

Exercise. Do 8 *battements tendus* with the *right* foot, closing in the *fifth* position *front*, and *fifth* position *back*, alternately.

Exercise with the Left Foot. Open the *left* foot to the *second* position, *pointe tendue*, and do 8 *battements tendus* with the *left* foot, closing in the *fifth* position *front*, and *fifth* position *back*, alternately.

ADAGE
4th & 5th ARABESQUES

You have already learnt the first, second, and third *arabesques*, we will now take the *fourth* and *fifth*.

The **fourth** *arabesque* is the same as the second *arabesque*, with the difference that the supporting knee is bent or *demi-plié* (see Plate IV).

The **fifth** *arabesque* is the same as the third *arabesque* with the difference that the supporting knee is bent or *demi-plié* (see Plate IV).

These two *arabesques* are usually taken facing corner 1, if the supporting leg is the *left*, or to corner 2, if the supporting leg is the *right*. In the illustrations the position is shown sideways for the sake of clearness.

Here is a new *adage*, known as *Deux Grands Ronds de Jambe en l'Air avec l'Arabesque*, which means *two large circles of the leg in the air with arabesque*.

Deux Grands Ronds de Jambe en l'Air avec l'Arabesque, as you will see when you come to do it, consists, broadly speaking, of

A $\begin{cases} \text{A \textit{développé à la quatrième devant en l'air}.} \\ \text{A \textit{grand rond de jambe en l'air en dehors}.} \end{cases}$

B   A repeat of A.

C $\begin{cases} \text{A \textit{développé à la seconde en l'air}.} \\ \text{A change in direction of the body so that the pose} \\ \text{becomes the \textit{first arabesque}.} \end{cases}$

Thus there are two *développés à la quatrième devant en l'air*, each followed by a *grand rond de jambe en l'air en dehors*, then a *développé à la seconde en l'air*, *relevé*, and change of direction.

DEUX GRANDS RONDS DE JAMBE EN L'AIR AVEC L'ARABESQUE

Stand erect in the centre of the room and face 2, with the head inclined to 3, the feet in the *fifth* position, *right* foot *front*, and the arms in the *fifth* position *en bas*.

1. *Grand plié* in the *fifth* position, then straighten both knees.

2. *Demi-plié* on both feet followed by a *relevé sur les demi-pointes*.

3. Lower the *left* heel to the ground.
   Raise the *right* foot *sur le cou-de-pied devant*.
   Turn to face 5 and bring the head erect.

4. **Développé à la quatrième devant en l'air** with the *right* foot.
   (*a*) As the *right* foot rises in a line with the side of the *left* knee—
   Raise the arms to the *fifth* position *en avant*.
   (*b*) As the foot is extended to the *fourth* position *front, en l'air*, pointing to 5—
   The arms remain in the *fifth* position *en avant*.

5. **Grand rond de jambe en l'air en dehors** with the *right* foot. That is:
   Keep the *right* foot extended, and the knee straight, and move the leg from the *fourth* position *front, en l'air—second* position *en l'air—fourth* position *back, en l'air*.
   As the foot moves from the *fourth* position *front, en l'air—second* position *en l'air—*
   Open the arms to the *second* position.
   Keep the arms extended as the foot moves from the *second* position, *en l'air—fourth* position *back, en l'air*.

6. **Développé à la quatrième devant en l'air** with the *right* foot.
   (*a*) As the *right* toe passes towards the *left* knee—
   Lower the arms to the *fifth* position *en bas*.
   (*b*) As the foot is extended to the *fourth* position *front, en l'air—*
   Raise the arms to the *fifth* position *en avant*.

7. **Grand rond de jambe en l'air en dehors** with the *right* foot.
The arms move exactly as in 5.
8. **Développé à la seconde en l'air** with the *right* foot.
(*a*) As the *right* toe passes towards the *left* knee—
Lower the arms to the *fifth* position *en bas*.
(*b*) As the right foot is extended to the *second* position, *en l'air*, pointing to 8—
Raise the arms to the *fifth* position *en avant* and open them to the *second* position.

9. Keep the *right* arm and foot pointing to 8, and the *left* arm pointing to 6, and quickly turn the body to the *left* so that it faces 6.
Turn the hands palm downwards, then slightly raise the *left* arm and lower the *right* arm.
The pose is in the *first arabesque*.
10. Retain the pose for an instant, then—
Lower the *right* foot to the *fifth* position *back*.
Lower the *left* heel to the ground.
Lower the arms to the *fifth* position *en bas*

Exercise of the Left Foot in Deux Grands Ronds de Jambe en l'air Avec l'Arabesque

Stand erect in the centre of the room and face 1, with the head inclined to 4, the feet in the *fifth* position, *left* foot *front*, and the arms in the *fifth* position *en bas*.

Repeat the whole of the exercise, reading *left* for *right*, and *vice versa*; while the wall and corner numbers stated above will now correspond to those directly opposite, that is: 8—6, 6—8.

ALLÉGRO

ASSEMBLÉ DE SUITE

This is executed in the same manner as *assemblé soutenu* (described on page 34), but do not straighten the knees between each *assemblé*, the *plié* you land in being the preparatory *plié* for the next *assemblé*. (Time value, two *assemblés de suite* to one *assemblé soutenu*.)

PAS DE BOURRÉE DESSOUS

Preparation. Stand erect in the centre of the room and face 5, with the head upright, the feet in the *fifth* position, *right* foot *front*, and the arms in the *fifth* position *en bas*.

Execution.

1. *Demi-pliez* on both feet and slide the *left* foot— straightening the knee—to the *second* position, *pointe tendue*; then open the leg a little further so that the *pointe* is about three inches off the ground. Open the arms to the *second* position.

2. (*a*) Bring the *left* foot to the *fifth* position back, both feet being *sur les demi-pointes*.
(*b*) Immediately the *left* foot meets the *right*, open the latter to the *second* position, *sur la demi-pointe*.
Lower *left* arm to form one half of the *first* position.

3. Carry the *left* foot in front of the *right*, so that the *pointe* is just off the ground, and immediately—
Lower both heels to the ground and *demi-pliez* on both feet.
Carry *left* arm to form one half of the *fifth* position *en bas*, then raise the hand close to the *right* breast.
As the *left* arm comes to the breast, turn the *right* hand palm downwards—keeping the arm in the *second* position—and move it slightly backwards so that it points to 4 (see Plate VI).
Incline the head so that you can see the *left* foot.

This step can also be begun with the *front* foot, but it is more usual to commence with the *back* foot.

DEMI-CONTRETEMPS

Preparation. Stand erect in the centre of the room and face 2, with the head upright, the feet in the *fourth* position, *left* foot *back*, and *pointe tendue*, and the arms in the *fifth* position *en bas*.

Execution.

1. (*a*) Spring upwards into the air off the *right* foot and bring the *left* foot *sur le cou-de-pied derrière*.
Turn the body to face 5.

(*b*) Come to the ground on the *right* foot—allowing
the knee to bend—and, keeping both knees bent,
slide the *left* foot through the first position to *fifth*
position *front*, to *fourth* position *front*, facing 1.
Turn the body to face 1.
Incline the head to 2.
The arms remain throughout in the *fifth* position *en
bas*.

NOTE.—This step consists of a *Temps levé* and a *Chassé
croisé*.

SOUBRESAUT

A *soubresaut* is a sudden leap or bound, rather like a
soussus off the ground.

Preparation.   Stand erect in the centre of the room and
face 5, with the head upright, the feet in the *fifth* position,
right foot *front*, and the arms in the *fifth* position *en bas*.

1. | *Demi-pliez* on both feet, and, keeping the feet drawn
together, spring up and slightly forward.
Raise arms to the *third arabesque*.
Incline the head to the *right*.

2. | Come to the ground in the *fifth* position, *right* foot
front, allowing the knees to bend.
Lower the arms to the *fifth* position *en bas*.

ENCHAÎNEMENTS
Three glissades changés and two petits changements.

This *enchaînement* is always done facing the audience
and on an imaginary line connecting the opposite walls of
the room; that is to say:

1. On the line 8—6, travelling to 6.
2. On the line 6—8, travelling to 8.

Preparation.   Stand erect in the centre of the room and
face 5, with the head upright and the feet in the *fifth* position, *right* foot *front*, and the arms in the *fifth* position *en
bas*.

Execution.

Do three *glissades*, beginning with the *right* foot and

Plate VII

Demi-Contretemps and Assemblé elancé

→ direction of Body
+ ; " " supporting Foot
→ ; " " extended "

The Positions of the Head

1	2	3	4	5
Head Erect	Head inclined to one side	Head turned to one side	Head raised	Head lowered

closing the *left* foot alternately in the *fifth* position *front*, *fifth* position *back*, and the *fifth* position *front*; the head is always inclined towards the foot that finishes in front. Conclude with two *petits changements* continuing the head movement.

Repeat to the other side.

Demi-contretemps and assemblé élancé, position écarteé.

Demi-contretemps means *half counter-beating*. At first acquaintance this *enchaînement* seems a little complicated, but, with a little care and application, you will be able to master it.

Preparation. Stand erect near 3, and face 2, with the head upright, the feet in the *fourth* position, *left* foot *back* and *pointe tendue*, and the arms in the *fifth* position *en bas*.

1. (a) Spring upwards into the air off the *right* foot and bring the left *sur le cou-de-pied derrière*.
Turn the body to face 5.

   (b) Come to the ground on the *right* foot—allowing the knee to bend—and, keeping the knee bent, slide the *left* foot through the *first* position, to *fifth* position *front*, and to *fourth* position *front*, facing 1.
Turn the body to face 1.
Incline the head to 2.

The arms remain throughout in the *fifth* position *en bas*.

Note.—This is the end of the *demi-contretemps*, which, you will notice, is composed of a *temps levé* and a *chassé croisé*.

2. (a) Slide the *right* foot to the *second* position, *en l'air*.
Open the arms to the *second* position.
Turn the head to 1, and slightly advance the *right* shoulder so that the position is *écarté* (the body faces 2).
Exactly as the *right* foot rises to the *second* position, *en l'air*—
Leap upwards into the air off the *left* foot.
While the body is in the air—

(*b*) Slightly bend both knees (a *plié à quart*) and bring together the flat of the toes of both feet.

(*c*) Come to the ground—allowing the knees to bend —with the feet in the *fifth* position, *right* foot *front*, and lower the heels to ground, then— Lower the arms to the *fifth* position *en bas*.

Perform this *enchaînement* twice or four times from 3—1, or from 4—2.

NOTE.—The movement of the arms in the *assemblé* should be so timed that the arms reach the full *second* position exactly as the leg comes to the *second* position, *en l'air*. *Élancé*, derived from *élancer*, to dart, means *darted*; therefore, when you jump upwards in the *assemblé*, travel upwards and sideways to 1.

See Plate VII for a diagram of this *enchaînement*.

Glissade derrière and assemblé dessus.

Preparation.   Stand erect in the centre of the room and face 5, with the head upright, the feet in the *fifth* position, *right* foot *front*, and the arms in the *fifth* position *en bas*.

   1. *Glissade derrière* with the *left* foot.
   2. *Assemblé dessus* with the *left* foot.

Perform this *enchaînement* four or eight times with alternate feet.

Three petits changements (en face) and two soubre-sauts (croisé) with arms in third *arabesque*.

Preparation.   Stand erect in the centre of the room and face 5, with the head upright, the feet in the *fifth* position, *right* foot *front*, and the arms in the *fifth* position *en bas*.

Execution.

   Do three *petits changements*, using head.
   (Arms remain in the fifth position *en bas*.)
   2. Do two *soubresauts* towards 1.
   Raise arms to the *third* arabesque, *right* arm up.
   During the two *soubresauts*, incline the head to *right*.
   Do this *enchaînement* 4 times.

Echappé Sauté à la Second, closing with beat.

Echappé is short for *temps échappé* meaning *escaping movement*. Thus the whole sentence means escaping movement jumped to the second position.

Preparation. Stand erect in the centre of the room and face 5, with the head upright, the feet in the *fifth* position, *right* foot *front*, and the arms in the *fifth* position *en bas*.

1. *Demi-pliez* on both feet and spring upwards into the air. Exactly as the feet leave the ground, instantaneously—

   Open the feet to the *second* position, a little wider than usual.
   Open the arms to the *demi-seconde* position.
   Come to the ground in the same position—allowing the knees to bend—and immediately—

2. Spring up and in, bring the *right* foot in front of the *left*, beating against it, open both feet slightly and come to the ground—allowing the knees to bend—with the feet in the *fifth* position *en bas*, *left* foot *front*.
   Incline the head slightly towards back foot as you spring out.

   Do this exercise 8 or 16 times in succession.

NOTE.—This exercise should be performed with the highest possible spring both out and in.

Temps levé, chassé, pas de bourrée dessous and relevé in fifth position.

Preparation. Stand erect in the centre of the room and face 5, with the head upright, the feet in the *fifth* position, *right* foot *front*, and the arms in the *fifth* position *en bas*.

Execution.

1. *Temps levé* on the *left* foot, leaving *right* foot fully stretched *sur le cou-de-pied devant*.

2. | *Chassé* to the *second* position.
   | Open the arms to the *demi-seconde* position.
   | Incline the head to the *right*.

3. | *Pas de bourrée dessous*.
   | Bring the arms to the *fifth* position *en bas*.
   | Incline the head to the *left*.

4. | *Relevé* in the *fifth* position.
   | Raise arms to the *fifth* position *en haut*, passing
   | through the *fifth* position *en avant*.
   | Incline the head to the *right*.

NOTE.—The complete *enchaînement* takes 4 bars of Waltz
music. Repeat the whole to the opposite side.

Petits Tours

Petits tours means *little turns*.

Preparation. Stand erect near 3 and facing 2, with the
head turned to the right, the feet in the *fifth* position, *right*
foot *front*, the finger-tips of the *left* hand resting on the *left*
shoulder and those of the *right* hand resting on the *right*
shoulder. The shoulders should be held well down and back,
the elbows pressed out and back, and the arms should
remain so placed through the exercise.

1. Step into the *second* position towards 1 on the *right*
demi-pointe, pivot on it to make a half turn to the *right*.

2. | Bring the *left* foot to a small *second* position, *sur la*
   | *demi-pointe*.
   | Turn the head to the *left*, so that you look at 1 as long
   | as possible.

3. | Pivot on the *left* foot, to make another half turn to
   | the *right*.
   | Bring the head sharply to the *right*.
   | The whole completes one turn.
   | Then step on the *right* foot towards 1 again, and
   | continue for 8 or more turns.

As you improve in this exercise, the steps should become
smaller and the pace quicker, but the turns should always be
done with due regard to the rhythm of the music.

Be sure to practise this exercise equally to *right* and *left*.